MANIFEST LIFE

How To Work In Harmony With The Law of Attraction

Richard Leyton

Manifest Life   Richard Leyton

ISBN 9798638556907

All rights reserved.

Manifest Life Copyright © 2020 by Richard Leyton.

Cover art by [Gestvlt](#)

Cover artwork copyright © 2020 by Inverse World Publishing

No part of this book may be reproduced or transmitted in any form or by any means, electronic or mechanical, including photocopying, recording, or by any information storage and retrieval system, without permission in writing from the publisher.

Table of Contents

Foreword

Introduction

Chapter 1 – Things You Should Know About The Law Of Attraction

Chapter 2 – What Is The Law Of Attraction?

Chapter 3 – Is The Law Of Attraction Real?

Chapter 4 – How To Use The Law Of Attraction

Chapter 5 – What The Mind Can Conceive, It Can Achieve

Chapter 6 – On The Verge Of Manifestation?

Chapter 7 – Why Manifestation Is Not Working For You?

Chapter 8 – Law Of Attraction Exercises

FOREWORD

The Law of Attraction, the most powerful force in the Universe. I am sure that it is something that by now you have heard a lot about, and it has either intrigued you; or you have had the same reaction to it as many people I come in contact with. It is something that you find to be pie in the sky, or just something that people who you suspect to be involved with the occult or some kind of voodoo spout, without taking the time to actually listen to what they have to say. If you are one of those people, there is no judgement here. I am simply glad that you allowed your mind to act on its curiosity, in order to take this opportunity to learn about this very important element that affects your life more than you realize, or wanted to before now.

In many ways, the Law of Attraction can be explained like gravity. It is something that is a part of everyone's life. A force or element that is always in motion, always in effect. With or without your knowledge, you are always in some state of creation at one point in time or another, over the course of your lifetime. You are constantly creating and attracting things into your reality every second of every day, whether you realize it or not. You are even going as far as to craft your own future with every thought and action; either deliberately or subconsciously. The Law of Attraction is something that is always constant. It is not an ability that you can just simply place on the back burner and decide to take a break from or stop altogether; because creation is something that is constantly in motion, as I said before. Creation never stops. Therefore, no matter what we do, we are always manifesting.

This is how understanding and unlocking the fundamental keys to how the Law of Attraction works. It is ultimately what will be the key to your success, and what will allow you to break through and reach your full potential. If you are someone who is looking to change their life by empowering themselves to craft the future they know they deserve, then first you must do as I did, and understand just how much of a role the Law of Attraction plays in all of our lives.

When I first came upon this concept, I will be the first to admit that I was a bit skeptical in the beginning. But over time, with the growing success of my business and now that I am a published author, I have come more and more to realize just how much I have been able, through harnessing the Law of Attraction, to bring this amount of success and abundance into my life and the lives of those around me.

    The first and foremost important thing about making the Law of Attraction work for you, is to understand that you should not be afraid to expect miracles. The Law of Attraction allows for so many infinite possibilities, abundance, and unlimited joy. It truly shows you just how much the Universe has no concept of difficulty. And, embracing this principle for yourself can utterly change your life in every way, as it did mine.

INTRODUCTION

In order to completely understand how the Law of Attraction works in your everyday life, we are going to go over several things that I have learned about these principles myself and that I feel need to be shared to benefit the rest of the world.

This book is for those of you who may at this moment in time be unfamiliar with the Law of Attraction, and desire to know more about it. Either simply because you are just curious, or you are looking for a way to take control of a life which you feel is currently out of your control. There is also a bit in here for those of you who are simply looking into why people practice the principles at all. After taking a look at what I have to offer, you may find that you also will desire to be one of those people. Joining the many of us who have taken a hold of the reins of our lives and are now fully in control of our destinies. Taking complete advantage of what the Universe has to offer us, and reaping all of the benefits.

To put it in very simple terms, the Law of Attraction is the ability to attract into your life whatever it is that you intend. This is known as the act of manifestation. In some circles this is where the term "Intention + Action = Magic" relates. This is what they are referring to. Many historical communities believe that the practice of the Law of Attraction was born out of the New Thought Movement, a philosophical movement that has been quoted as saying many times, *"Infinite Intelligence is everywhere, spirit is the totality of real things, true human selfhood is divine, divine thought is a force for good, sickness originates in the mind, and 'right thinking' has a 'healing effect"*. To boil this down even further into even simpler terms, they are saying that the Law of Attraction teaches us that through people and their thoughts is formed pure energy; which can be either positive or negative. An individual's thoughts are the most powerful influences on a person's life. And, everyone's thoughts are directly connected with the Universe's energy.

The majority of our thoughts as human beings can be classified as one of two types of thought patterns. You have either limiting or self-destructive, negative, thoughts. Or, empowered and adaptive, positive, thoughts. Our thoughts produce energy, which is either aligned or misaligned with the Universal Law that controls everything. This law ultimately controls what a person receives into their life, whether it be good or bad. Hence, the saying "Like energy attracts like energy," and a person can always work on increasing their level of good energy, or vibrations as many people call it. This you will find will improve various aspects of your life. For instance, things like your health, your finances, your personal relationships, spirituality, and so on and so forth. However, should a person's individual disposition be that of a negative vibration, the Law of attraction teaches us the ability to rewire or reframe these thought processes using cognitive rewiring practices such as personal daily affirmations, creative visualization, and often times the most effective meditation and hypnosis.

    Now whether you are a passionate believer or a total skeptic of the New Thought Movement, there is certainly no denying the presence of thousands of experts all over the world, who can attest with scientific rationalism, that there is fact behind such principles as the Law of Attraction and similar ideas. Just think of the principle of deep meditation for a moment and how that has proven to be effective in many cases. When it comes to a person being able to heal themselves of things like cancer, learning to walk again, regaining their sense of smell, and even re-fusing their own brain back together after it was split completely in two by a serious head injury. It has been cited by many medical and psychiatric studies, that the human mind does in fact conform to its function to respond automatically through the subconscious, to the Law of Attraction. Have you ever noticed that when you are in a room with several people who are anxious, you find that you take on their anxiety, without even intending to? It just happens. Just like when you are in a room with a whole bunch of people who are panicking or are just simply afraid, you will find that more often than not you yourself will also become afraid; due to the energy that is the most prevalent in the room. And of course, these principles and theories also apply greatly to happiness and the anticipation of reward. Scientists have found that when an individual's brain lights up in the centers of the mind which correspond to emotional responses like someone's happiness or laughter, they reflect in others as well. Almost like a contagious effect. The reason for this is, simply because it is. You have been infected by the happy energy they are exuding, which caused their laughter and yours as well. All of these connections support the theory of the Law of Attraction. Because, underpinning all of these theories and ideas is the concept of connection. We are all universally connected to each other inside and out, as we are with God and the universe themselves. Thus, making the intentions of our feelings and actions, a critical part of the equation when it comes to attracting what exactly it is that we desire into our lives.

CHAPTER ONE
Things You Should Know About The Law Of Attraction

Law of Attraction, or LOA, practitioners, while similar to those who adhere to a religious doctrine or other belief system, often seek to clarify any misconceptions about the practice. And rightfully so. Many times, they also strive to inform and perhaps guide others down their new life path.

Here are ten reasons I personally believe more people should know about the Law of Attraction.

1. Universal Knowledge

Universal knowledge is far more comprehensive than our own. It is estimated that the universe itself originated approximately 13.82 billion years ago. In that time, forces beyond human understanding designed and implemented laws that continue to govern the cosmos. Meaning, human beings in their mere 200,000 years or so on Earth have only scratched the surface of the Universe's secrets. In other words, the universe possesses wisdom far beyond human understanding. But more importantly, once we take the time to learn how, we can communicate with this wisdom.

2. Resistance is Common

Many LOA practitioners face the same resistance we all do when first introduced to a new way of thinking. Merely learning and understanding the concept of the Law of Attraction, or being inspired by its teachings and methods is not quite the same as truly believing. It is common and healthy to question things. In fact, this is something that the LOA itself not only adequately addresses, but also encourages. Because we are all creatures of comfort, we are more likely to continue to do what seems more natural to us, even if the result is ultimately harmful. So when we are introduced to a new habit or way of life, it may seem scary or uncomfortable. This is how you know you are on the right track, when you feel there has been an uncharacteristic shift.

3. The ability to evaluate and work on unproductive thought patterns to change our reality

In order to change our thoughts and current reality, we must first be able to evaluate and work on our world as we know it. We do this by unpacking and examining our current thought patterns and beliefs. What I mean by "work" in this sense is taking the time to acknowledge any inner conflict or turbulence or negative thinking sequences and addressing them. Once you have taken the time to address each of them, only then can you begin to replace them with more productive patterns of thought and belief.

4. Trust in the perfection of Divine Timing

Divine timing really is everything. The Law of Attraction teaches that there is a plan for everyone's life, and that the manifestation of this plan requires patience. Furthermore, the intentions we have set for our life may not come to fruition until we acquire certain knowledge that the Universe believes is necessary for us to move forward.

5. The Universe Requires Our Participation

Many predominant religious practices base their methodology on a "complete surrender" to a creator, while others forbid certain acts, referring to them as sinful. The Law of Attraction teaches no such dogma. Instead, it does compel individuals to make their intentions known to the universe. Establishing a belief in co-creation, or a partnership with the cosmic energy in order to achieve one's goals.

6. E-Motion, Energy-In-Motion, Do not fake your emotions

The Law of Attraction encourages the honest expression of emotions in order to acquire the things that we seek. A founding element of LOA is that the Universe sends back the energy it receives, and as such it is a good thing for us to wait until we are happy or at peace before making our intentions known. Or creating circumstances in which we are happy or at peace.

7. LOA is not for the purpose of manipulation

There is a small minority within the Law of Attraction community who believe that the Universal Law can be used to manipulate or control other people. This is a viewpoint which is not only a gross inaccuracy, but also an insult to the universe as well as those of us who use LOA's methods for the purpose of bettering ourselves and the world around us.

8. The Art of Letting Go

Learning to let go is a necessary skill to acquire, when practicing the Law of Attraction. Since what we receive from the universe heavily depends upon the energy we emit, releasing our internal conflicts is a skill that can and must be learned. There are many people who practice LOA who are minimalists, and they don't require much love. And, as such, they are less vulnerable to being hurt by external influences because they have mastered the skill of letting go.

9. The Spiritual Support System

There are many within the LOA community who are very spiritual people. This deep sense of spirituality greatly involves a belief in the immaterial, especially good forces such as angels and spiritual guides. These forces provide a reassurance to someone on their path and reinforce their faith. A strong pillar of LOA.

10. Everything that happens in life is not your fault

One common misconception people have about the Law of Attraction is that it teaches people to believe everything wrong in their life is of their own doing. However, this completely untrue. What the Law of Attraction does explain is transcendence. The belief that the Universe helps us to learn and grow through our circumstances and thus fulfill our destiny. So it is important to keep in mind that even though to some degree we have the ability to control our own reality, it is important to acknowledge there are still many things about our life that remain out of our control. And that some things are indeed still beyond human comprehension.

CHAPTER TWO
What is the Law of Attraction?

Quite simply put, the Law of Attraction is the ability to attract into our lives whatever we are focusing on the most. It is believed that regardless of age, nationality, or religious inclination, we are all susceptible to the laws which govern the Universe; including the Law of Attraction. It is the Law of Attraction which uses the power of the mind to translate whatever is in our thoughts and materialize them into reality. In layman's terms, all thoughts will eventually turn into something material. If you focus on negative doom and gloom you will remain under a cloud. Just as if you instead focus on positive thoughts and have goals that you are aiming to achieve, you will find a way to achieve them with great effect.

This is why the Universe is such an infinitely beautiful place. The Law of Attraction dictates that whatever can be imagined and held in the mind's eye is achievable, if you take action on a plan to get to where you want to be.

The Law of Attraction to many people is considered to be one of the biggest mysteries in life. There are very few people who are fully aware of how much of an impact the Law of Attraction has on their day to day life. Whether we are practicing it knowingly or unknowingly, every second of our existence, we are acting as human magnets sending out our thoughts and emotions, and thus attracting back more of what we have put out into the Universe. Unfortunately, so many of us are still blind to the potential that is locked deep inside of us. Consequently, it is all too easy to leave your thoughts and emotions unchecked. Essentially, living your life on auto-pilot, or asleep so to speak in the passenger seat of your own life. This sends out the wrong thoughts and attracts more unwanted circumstances, causing you to stay in this seemingly never-ending cycle of "bad luck". Having said this, discovering that the Law of Attraction is at work within your life should be a great cause for celebration. Once the power of attraction has been understood by you it is now no longer a secret. Plus, you are now officially awake, now that you have learned how to effectively apply these to your everyday life, and your future is now entirely yours to create. There is no limit to what you can do with it!

However, before you begin to embark on this incredible journey towards the true enlightenment, it is important to first understand that you can apply it to your life and it can be effective, if the correct tools are used. The practices and beliefs in this law have been igniting the lives of great people throughout the course of history. Hundreds of years ago, the Law of Attraction was first thought to have been taught to a man by the immortal Buddha. It is believed he wanted it to be known that "what you have become is what you have thought." With the spread of this concept to western culture, also came the term "Karma." A belief that is popular throughout numerous societies and religions all over the world. Over the centuries it has been a common understanding amongst many that what you give out to the world or Universe, be it anger, hate, love, or happiness; these are the things that will be returned to you throughout your life in the end. Pretty simple and easy to follow concept, right? It demonstrates that the idea of the power of attraction is not new whatsoever. Proof of praise for the Laws of Attraction and its main principles are present in the teachings of many other civilizations and religious groups the ages. For instance, in Proverbs 23:7, it reads, "As a man thinks in his heart so is he." All recorded and taught in many different ways. However, still there for all of humanity to find, if they are just willing to look.

CHAPTER THREE
Is The Law of Attraction Real?

As I have previously discussed, the Law of Attraction and its principles have been displayed throughout history. And a great many women and men who have left their mark on the world have shown the it to be one of the most powerful forces on earth. Many of our well-beloved poets, artists, scientists and great thinkers such as Shakespeare, Blake, Emerson, Newton, and Beethoven; all conveyed this message through their great and many works. There has also been many modern advocates for the Law of Attraction as well. These include, but are not limited to, people such as Oprah Winfrey, Jim Carrey, and Denzel Washington, just to name a few.

The most challenging part of acknowledging and accepting the truth about what the Law of Attraction has to offer is coming to the realization that every single one of your decisions in life, both good and bad, has been shaped by you alone. For many people, this can be a bit of a bitter pill to swallow. Especially, if you feel that you or your loved ones have been dealt some particularly tough blows in life. Like, bad health, rocky financial situations, etc.

However, once you have come to a true understanding of the key elements behind the Law of Attraction, you can rest renewed with the hope and courage in the overwhelming wisdom that you are free to take charge of your life, and free yourself forever from the cycle of fear, worry, or negativity that has held you back for so long.

If you find yourself still a bit skeptical, there is a science behind the Law of Attraction that proves it to be more fact than fiction. The work of quantum physicists during recent years has helped to shine a greater light on the incredible impact that the power of the mind has on our lives and the universe in general. The more that this idea is explored by scientists and other great minds alike, the better the understanding we have on just how significant of a role the brain plays in shaping our lives, and the perception we have of the world around us. It does not matter if you do not ever come to possess a thorough understanding of the quantum physics behind the Law of Attraction. However, this does not mean that we all cannot enjoy the many benefits that this generous law can offer us and allow us to have, if we are willing to just take hold of it.

As physicists come to supply us with more and more information regarding the law itself, the more we can simply rejoice in the truly freeing and empowering realization that we are the creators and authorities of our life and the energies we are all made of.

So, be happy, for the universe is always on your side. The more time you dedicate to learning and cultivating your ability to use the Law of Attraction effectively in your own life, the more fulfilling and rewarding your life will be. There are no restrictions! Open your mind and enjoy the natural abundance of the universe. The best thing about desire is allowing yourself to have it.

CHAPTER FOUR
How to Use the Law of Attraction

Once we have come to the understanding of the astounding possibilities that life has to offer us, we can also come to realize that we are our own life's artists. We are creating pictures of our intended life, then making choices, and taking actions that will realize what we envisaged.

So what if you don't like the picture? Change it! It really is as simple as that!

Life is a blank canvas of possibility; you are in control of what the finished picture will look like. It really is that simple. No catches. All laws of nature are completely perfect and the Law of Attraction is no different. No matter what you are looking to have, or achieve, or be in life, if you can hold onto an idea and see it for yourself in your mind's eye, you can make it yours to have... with some effort on your part, of course. For only through unwavering faith and extraordinary effort can miracles happen.

Here are just a few areas in daily life that people seek to improve by utilizing The Law Of Attraction.

1. Manifest Love And Relationships With The Law Of Attraction

"The beginning of love is at the end of resistance."
                                                            - Danielle Light

With new relationships being formed every single day, it is not surprising that this is a common goal. Many people wish to meet the love of their lives. But can The Law Of Attraction help your love life?

The short answer? Yes. You can manifest love with a particular person by navigating universal law pathways to gravitate them into your space.

I know that sometimes it can feel like everyone else around you has already figured out how to make the whole "relationship thing" work and you are the only one left out in the cold or dark, who can't find the right one. This can be very emotionally and mentally exhausting for many people to deal with repeated break-ups, bad dates, and trying to manifest love but never seeming to have any luck. Not to mention the constant battle of loneliness, lowered self-esteem due to multiple rejections, and constantly yearning for a better life that includes someone else. Sound familiar? It is a perfectly normal inclination to just want to throw in the towel sometimes. Perhaps you have decided to resign yourself to the single life, in spite of the fact you still feel that deep yearning within your soul to find love. However, the good news is that there are many Law Of Attraction techniques and exercises that can increase your confidence, charisma and overall subconscious willingness to receive love. No matter how desperate or fruitless your experiences have been up until now, it is still possible to manifest what you desire. Even manifesting the specific type of person you are looking for. But first you must dig a little deeper into how the Law of Attraction can work to help you understand why you are struggling so hard to manifest a long-lasting love.

When it comes to manifesting your soulmate, it is crucial to first and foremost gain an understanding of why it is that all of your attempts up until this point have seemingly failed. You must first realize that everyone's journey to finding love differs from person to person. Except, there are many common factors at play that have a tendency to act as road blocks on your way to creating the romance you, and all of us, deserve to have in our lives. For instance, on your quest of self-diagnosis you may discover a few of the following things to be true.

A. You have subconsciously given up or shut yourself down

This tends to happen after being hurt and finding yourself frequently disappointed. So, in order to defend yourself against what you perceive to be future heart break, you build walls and close yourself off through processes of self-sabotage, that you believe are defense mechanisms. However, this unfortunately also shuts you off from potential love as well, because you are sending out signals to the Universe that you don't want a relationship.

B. You have left things unfinished

It can be very difficult to attract love into your near future reality when you constantly keep one foot in the past. Or continue to live there altogether. Maybe you have never taken the time to fully unpack a past traumatic relationship and heal from that experience by allowing yourself the opportunity to create your own closure. Causing you to find it even harder to let go of this old partner. So, you are unable to manifest something new into your reality because you have not fully exorcised the ghost of this other person from your mind or life.

C. A loss of faith

Since you have been looking for love for what you feel like is such a long time, you may find yourself losing the belief that you will ever find it, or that there is such a thing as a soul mate. This may also cause you to be tempted to settle for a relationship that is not as beneficial to you as a healthy one would be, because you feel like an "okay" relationship is all the love you deserve. Rather than committing to the mission to draw your love to yourself because you are tired and it looks like work. So, you resign yourself to the mindset of, "my need for love is not starving because it is at least surviving on crumbs, and that's better than nothing."

All of these thought patterns are sure fire ways to sabotage yourself when it comes to manifesting the love you desire into your life. This is why it is so important to do your best to rewire your mind to develop more productive thought patterns that will actually attract the love you want rather than deflect it.
The best place to begin this journey is to start by understanding love is not something that has to be sought. It is everywhere in everything. Especially, yourself. Just as happiness is not a place that you go, it is always with you, whether you choose to see it or not. Or success is not something that you have to achieve, it is simply preparation meeting opportunity, both you can provide for yourself by preparing yourself for the thing you wish to be successful in then giving yourself the opportunity to apply the preparation. It is all about intention. If you believe that the endeavor is worth it, you will apply the appropriate amount of energetic intention.
The key message you must engrain within yourself is that you have to begin drawing love to yourself through genuine intention. What this means is that you need to learn to align yourself with the most effective vibrational frequency to attract love into your life, rather than deterring it and creating further disappointment. In order to do this, you need to cultivate a clear sense of what you are actually trying to accomplish with your aim to manifest love, because many of us just go through life without refining our concept of what love means to us on a personal level. The key to manifesting a desired result is through complete specificity. Terms like "love" are general and unspecific because they mean something different to

everyone, as well as possessing varying degrees. It is like saying that you want your water to be hot, well how hot do you want it? Would you like it to be at a simmer? Or would you like it to boil? These are principles that must be considered when taking a journey like this, for it is very difficult for the Universe to help bring us the love we desire if we don't actually know what we want specifically.

Essentially, you need to make the decision that you really want to attract this life partner. Then, truly commit to the idea of spending the rest of your life with this person. Making this commitment may involve processing old wounds (e.g. via journaling or therapy). Hopefully, the past can be left behind and you can opt to embrace hope instead of fear.

Once you've made your decision, a big part of understanding how to manifest love with a specific person lies in getting a clear sense of what it is about this person that makes you believe that looking for love with them will truly make you happy. As such, part of making a manifestation commitment involves beginning to analyze yourself in a new, deeper way.

Ask yourself the following about your needs and desires in your quest to find love:

* What 5-10 words would you use to describe what you really want in a partner?
* What personality traits in another person not only attract love from you but also help to bring out the very best in you?
* How do you want to be treated by a partner? When looking for love, what are the behaviors that you will simply never tolerate?
* What are your deepest, most heartfelt passions in life?
* What do you consider to be your life's mission? Plus, what sort of partner can be a teammate on the road to achieving this goal?

When you understand the answers to these types of questions about manifesting your soulmate, your mind and heart begin to focus on trying to find love that is based on true mutual understanding and excitement. You can do all kinds of creative techniques to bolster the designing of your life partner. For example, Law of Attraction experts recommend daily visualization exercises in which you conjure up a vivid sense of what your life partner would be like. Meanwhile, you can also create a dream board that represents all the traits you're looking for and your image of how this relationship will improve your life.

However, an important cautionary note is that you absolutely must set realistic expectations. It's not possible to manifest love with a "perfect" person because there is no such thing as a perfect person. You have to be willing to find love with someone who is perfect for you but who has some flaws and difficulties nonetheless.

Next, you should learn how to reconnect with your true self. There's an old cliché that claims you can't love others unless you love yourself. However, there is truth in this saying. It can have a major impact on whether you're able to successfully manifest love. Specifically, you attract love with people who are aligned with your vibrational state. So if you are down on yourself or lack confidence, you often find love only with people who treat you poorly and fail to recognize your worth. Therefore, looking for love with real intention requires you to form a deeper, more profound and accepting connection with yourself.

Whether or not you feel it right now, everyone contains the essence of love. This is an infinite resource that you can draw on at all times... Not just when you're looking for love.

Here are some tips that will help you develop this self-love, enabling you to manifest love with your soul mate:

Become the person you want to attract. Take another look at the life partner you designed according to all the key qualities you value. Next, try to think of how you can cultivate those precise traits in yourself. For example, if ambition is on your list, ask yourself how you can work harder to achieve your goals (in work, and in life more broadly).

Make time for self-care. Learning how to connect with yourself has a lot to do with tuning into your own needs, then consequently meeting those needs. When you make a habit of this, you're much more able to attract love with someone who will nurture you. One way to ensure you take better care of yourself while you're looking for love is to set aside an hour a day where you commit to pursuing a hobby you love! This should be no matter what other, more "productive" things you could be doing.

Challenge your limiting beliefs. As with all Law of Attraction work, trying to manifest love requires that you look at the underlying assumption that holds you back. In this case, limiting beliefs that might block you from finding love. Try to write them down first. Then identify where they came from. Most importantly, write down a contradictory belief that you can then turn into a daily affirmation.

Now, it's time to let the universe know you're truly ready to manifest your soulmate. Simply coming into a more positive vibrational alignment can certainly help you find love. However, there's also a specific process you can follow to help you attract love more quickly. These steps will open you up to a soul-deep connection with the specific person you want to find love with:

* Set a clear intention. First, write something down until you get the words right. Then when you're happy, say them out loud as you look at yourself in the mirror. Some examples include "I am ready to manifest love and I open my heart to my one true soulmate" and "My mind is clear, my heart is open, and I am ready to welcome my soulmate in."

* Affirm your belief in your soulmate. While you've already worked hard to combat limiting beliefs and create a clear image of the person you want to be with, you make it easier for the Universe to send that person your way if you constantly stay connected to your belief that they exist. Try daily affirmations (written or spoken) like "I am looking for love, and my soulmate is on their way to me". Plus, "Nothing will stop me from receiving the love of my soulmate."

* Multi-sensory visualization. Take your creative visualization further and begin to spend longer daily sessions imagining every aspect of being with your soulmate. The stronger this mental image, the stronger the pull you will exert on them. Think not only about how they will look but also how they will sound, smell and feel. You might also try picturing significant moments in your life. For example, visualize events like sharing a bed for the first time, getting married or having children.

Lastly, trust and understand this is a process. As you work to manifest your soulmate, the final stage of your journey to attract love involves cultivating patience. Embrace this sense of peace as you accept that the Universe can – and will – give you what you need. Although you've been focusing on how to manifest love with a specific person, looking for love through law of attraction techniques rests on your ability to trust that the Universe knows exactly what kind of partner can help you manifest love that lasts. Don't fret about when you're going to find your soulmate. But rather, rest easy in the knowledge that you will find them at the perfect time. You might not find love quite where and when you expected it. So you must keep an open mind and be alert to signs from the universe. These might come in the form of coincidences, repeated imagery, or chance meetings.

Believe that your intuition can tell whether such potential signs are significant.

Living "as if" can be a powerful way to help yourself to manifest love. What this means is that you should try to live every day not as though you're looking for love, but as though you've already found it!

Embrace self-love and dress as you would if you were spending time with your partner. Try to make space for them in your home. See yourself as a person with a loving soulmate and a bright future, and make plans accordingly.

Remember that now you know exactly what you want, you will be certain when you find love. When you manifest love with a soulmate, there is no ambiguity. You will just know you have found the right one.

Finally, start every day by tuning into your heart. Visualize being with the one you love, and let a warm, golden glow fill your chest. This is the energy that will propel you through the day on exactly the right frequency to attract love.

Take that feeling wherever you go. Be aware that your soulmate is always with you, even when you have yet to meet them. In this way, it is entirely possible to attract your real soulmate by utilizing The Law Of Attraction.

2. Attract Money And Wealth Using The Law Of Attraction

"Always remember, money is a servant; you are the master."
- Bob Proctor

Another common goal across the world is financial abundance. Wealth brings along it's obvious benefits to your life. Money can put a roof over your head and food on the table. Similarly, it has the ability to provide for your family and friends.

Unfortunately, many of us have troubled relationships with the idea of wealth. It certainly has connotations of greed and vanity. In order to attract money, we need to banish these negative thought patterns. A key aspect of The Law of Attraction is this idea that positivity breeds positivity. Therefore, you can learn how to harness positive money habits easily with help from visualization tools and techniques.

It's entirely possible to manifest wealth using the law of attraction. In many of best Law of Attraction money stories, financial success is the gateway to a huge number of other forms of success.

Whether you want to wine and dine your dream partner, start a new business, travel the world or build your confidence, some extra cash certainly can't hurt. Even if abundance isn't your main

manifestation goal, you'll surely benefit from attracting more money into your life regardless.
To do so, first you need to get into the right mind set, and you can do that once you master these six easy exercises.

Step 1. To Attract Money, Focus On Abundance

Often top of the list of Law of Attraction money tips, this exercise is predicated on the core Law of Attraction premise that you attract more of what you focus on.
So, if you spend more time focusing on the abundance you have, more could come your way. There are many ways to do this. For example:
* Keep a journal and make a daily habit of noting down 1-5 things you're grateful to have.
* Close your eyes for 3-5 minutes, spending all the time inhabiting your deepest feelings of gratitude for the abundance in your life.

Step 2. Flip The Script

When you're trying to attract abundance, your inner critic will often tell you that you can't. Sometimes, it will even tell you that you don't deserve to be wealthy.
Whenever a negative thought like this arises, immediately flip it around and focus on the opposite. For example, when you worry "I don't think I'll ever be successful enough to make money", firmly tell yourself "Everyone can be successful enough to make huge amounts of money".
If necessary, use a thought-stopping technique like saying the word "Stop" out loud or picturing a red stop sign.

Step 3. Spend In Alignment With Your Values

Another of the best ways to attract money is to ensure you spend the wealth you have on things that really matter. When you live in a way that aligns with your values, you develop a much more positive relationship with money. And when you view money in a positive, loving way, you'll attract more money instantly!
And if you're not sure what you value, do the following:
1. Write down the five most important experiences of your life.
2. Write 5 words that describe each.
3. Ask yourself: what common themes emerge? These are your key values.

Step 4. Face Facts

Manifesting wealth isn't just about connecting money with happiness. It's also about looking at the reality of your financial situation and acting accordingly. So, be honest with yourself. Look at all your finances, including debts. Don't be afraid to reach out for help if you need it. Friends, family, and financial advisers can all help you draw up a plan to improve the situation.
If you don't have abundance today, that's okay. Remind yourself that it's not possible to get to where you want to go unless you engage with the truth of where you are right now.

Step 5. Smell Money
While it might sound strange at first, you'll be better at using the Law of Attraction for money and wealth if you connect with the smell of money. When you do this, you align your own vibration with wealth and abundance. As you do this, imagine yourself having all the wealth you need. Don't think about why you want money, or how you wish you had more money. Let your brain believe you are fully abundant, right now.
Another exercise involves smelling of money, and conditions your brain to set itself to tasks that result in the inflow of money.
First get yourself an expensive scent. It could be a perfume, aftershave or lotion; basically anything that makes you smell good to yourself and others, and is among the priciest in its class. Next, you have to set yourself a monetary target to meet, which upon completion, unlocks the use of the money scent. So, if your target was a hundred dollars, then you don't get to smell like money until you've made a hundred dollars. Quite torturous, yes, but only to those who do not wish to smell like money. Its about getting in the right mindset, doing the work and letting the Law Of Attraction cover the rest.
These are quick and easy exercises. However, when done often, they can reset old negative beliefs about money, ones that are holding you back currently.

Step 6. Banish Fear Of Success

Many people accidentally self-sabotage. So, you might on some level be afraid of what will happen if you attract money!

Manifest Life
Richard Leyton

1. Write down all the reasons you might be afraid to be abundant. For example, you might write "What if people only use me for my wealth?" or "What if I'm not happy, even when I'm rich?".
2. For each fear, think about where it comes from. Did someone from your past give you this message? Is it coming from your social setting? Note the source.
3. Finally, write a reply to each worry. For example, "I'll still know true friends from false friends no matter how wealthy I am".

Perhaps you're already practicing meditation, or maybe you're just thinking about trying it for the first time. Regardless, a guided meditation to attract money can be done by everyone.

It's a wonderful way of tuning your mind into the reality of your abundance, creating positive emotions about wealth and giving you a more vivid picture of what it will be like to manifest your goal.

Plus, meditation has dozens of other scientifically proven benefits, ranging from stress management to increased empathy, lower blood pressure, and better mental health.

You can't manifest huge sums of money overnight, but you can create the preconditions for wealth virtually overnight. We'll take you through a basic money meditation, step by step.

Think of the following as an "attract money now" meditation (ideally performed before sleep so that the messages can be readily absorbed into your subconscious):

1. Meditations begin with finding a comfortable, quiet place where you won't be disturbed. Sit down cross-legged, or in a chair with your feet touching the ground.
2. Take 5 deep breaths, inhaling and exhaling to a count of ten each time. As you do this, release all tension from your body. Imagining it dissipating at the top of your head, then work your way down to your neck, chest, waist, legs, and feet.
3. When you're fully relaxed, imagine your body warming up and being filled with a warm, golden light.
4. After a few minutes pass, imagine money raining down on you. Imagine it adding up to millions of dollars. Imagine it filling your rooms and the rooms of your neighbors. There is enough for everyone.
5. Let yourself feel joyful and fulfilled. After another few minutes of bathing in this happiness, slowly open your eyes.

Once you're used to this attract money meditation, you can move on to repeat it twice or three times a day, not just before sleep.

Money Affirmations For Wealth And Abundance:

Aimed at harnessing the Law of Attraction, money affirmations can quickly help to focus your heart and mind on your goal. They are simple phrases that contain powerful messages of happiness and success. Try the following affirmations for wealth and abundance. Saying them into a mirror before you start your day can be especially effective.

* *"I love money. Money is good."*
* *"I am attracting more money each day."*
* *"I am ready to receive all the wealth I deserve."*
* *"There is no limit to how much money I can attract."*
* *"I value money and am attracting more and more of it into my life."*
* *"I will always have exactly the amount of money I need."*
* *"Earning money is easy for me."*
* *"I know I can succeed in attracting wealth, and in achieving all my goals."*
* *"I live a successful, abundant, joyful life."*
* *"Every day, I magnetically attract more wealth."*

3. Improve Your Mental And Physical Health
"Mens sana in corpore sano"
                              – Latin phrase

The saying above translates to *"a healthy mind in a healthy body"*, and rightly so. A healthy mind creates a healthy body, but the truth is with busy work routines, commitments to friends and family and general everyday life, we sometimes neglect our own personal health. Whilst utilizing The Law Of Attraction cannot purely substitute a healthy diet, exercise and regular doctor checkups, it can promote a vast range of benefits for your mental, spiritual and physical health.

Our minds are continually subject to bombardment with messages from society. These messages remain insistent on the inevitable toll that aging can have on us all. They inform us that we need to diet. They teach us about all of the illnesses and dangers to our health. You must reject these ideas immediately! You and you alone are in control of what happens to your body. Maintain a strong, positive mind and then record your results.

In using the visualization tools and Law of Attraction exercises that are available to us, we can become the masters of our minds. We soon come to filter which thoughts we choose to listen to;

controlling the amount of stress we permit into our bodies. As a result, we quickly find ourselves on the path to achieving complete health and feelings of well-being.

Training your brain to see the positive in everything allows room for mental growth and happiness, which in turn can improve your physical health. Similarly, taking time for self-care can help combat a range of mental illnesses.

The responsibility of maintaining a healthy and age-resistant body is entirely within our hands. Our physical health and outward age are simply a manifestation of our inner thoughts and beliefs, whether they are consciously or unconsciously thought, which gives us complete power over whether we choose to accept premature aging or illness into our bodies or not.

One of the greatest things that we can learn from the Law of Attraction is that within our minds we have the power to choose our thoughts, whether positive or negative. This can have an impact on our physical and mental health too. Mind over matter is possible and by opening up our minds we can all develop exceptional healing abilities of our very own.

It has already been acknowledged within modern medicine that the 'placebo effect' is very real. This demonstrates the magnitude of importance that the mind has in the physical recovery of the body. It has conveyed to the world the marvelous capabilities of the mind in its ability to convince itself and the body into a state of total health, without any external intervention.

However, this is not to say that conventional forms of medicine should not also be adhered to. Modern medicine and medical intervention have a crucial part to play in the healing process. However, when combined with the remarkable capabilities of the mind, healing can be accelerated and will encourage long-lasting health.

Whether we are aware of it or not, the powers of attraction are continually within play. Therefore, whatever is going on within our mental psyche is often being reflected in the condition of our physical body. This is why any symptoms or ailments that our body displays should be received gratefully, as they are a warning to us that something needs to be changed.

A. Eliminate Stress

The single most common cause of any emotional or physical illness is always the result of some form of stress that our mind has experienced. Build-ups of negativity which have been left unchecked will continue to grow until they eventually spill over into some physical sign of illness. As a result, eliminating all forms of physiological stress and refusing to allow any room in your mind for dwelling on the discomfort or worry of bad health can allow your body the room and time to eliminate itself of all illnesses.

There should be no room for illness or aging in a body where the mind sees itself as absolutely perfect.

B. Improve Your Self-Image And Utilize Positive Thinking

Taking charge of our bodies also means taking control over our self-image, including the issue of weight and our attitudes towards weight loss. The predicament of weight-loss and the long battle that you may or may not have waged with your body throughout your lifetime, has become more and more complex, as our society has become more fixated with what we eat and the way that we look.

Do you constantly find yourself fixating on your weight? Are you disheartened by the sight that greets you whenever you take a look in the mirror? If this is so and you are looking to lose weight and acquire your dream body with minimal effort on your part, then you need to ensure that your thoughts are in check first and foremost.

Whatever thoughts you choose to fill your head with, including 'fat or skinny thoughts', will be reflected in great abundance. When you obsess about your weight, this can only lead to more 'fat thoughts' and increased weight gain. Unbeknown to many people, countless 'weight-watchers' will go on numerous diets and spend hours dedicated to fretting about their waistline, unknowingly contributing towards their weight the entire time.

Notice the problem? Then focus on exchanging 'fat thoughts' for 'thin' ones (or vice versa) immediately if this is what you want. Once you begin to train your thoughts, you can discover and experience how positive thinking boosts health.

Your body is perfect. Remember this and remain focused on the love that you feel for your body right now.

4. Get Fit, Lose Weight And Have A More Mindful Diet

"Emotional eating can be a source of shame and frustration, but there are ways to beat it. The trick is to learn more about your triggers and develop a pattern of mindful eating that replaces the old, self-destructive pattern of being an emotional eater."

Similar to the goal mentioned earlier, losing weight can be a very demotivating process for a number of reasons, and can often lead to the formation of self-harming habits like emotional eating. However, this need not be the case. Positive thinking can really help eliminate binge eating and a lack of motivation.

A more mindful approach to eating can also reveal a lot about your body and appetite. In this way, visualization tools and techniques can really be handy when trying to get fit.

5. Increase Your Self-Confidence And Combat Anxiety

Mental health can really impact your physical health and wellbeing. The Law Of Attraction focuses on this idea of self-confidence and faith in the universe. Therefore, you need to let go off all feelings of doubt in yourself in order to effectively decrease any levels of stress as soon as you can.

Of all the negative emotions that can reduce your capacity for attracting what you desire, fear is one of the most potent. Are you anxious, stressed and frightened when you think about everything that could go wrong in life?

If so, you're not alone! However, you do need to develop a strategy for changing this mindset. Fear holds you back and keeps you focused on the idea of lack, while love fills you with positivity and heightens your energy vibration in a way that makes your manifestation abilities much more powerful.

Here are things you can start doing immediately if you want to learn how to transform fear into love.

Step 1: Understand Your Fears

First, you need to analyze your worries and find the root of your unhappiness. This isn't an easy process. It can be quite scary actually. Many prefer to just ignore their fears because they don't want to look deeper into them. But in order to become emotionally stronger, we need to address the problem, not hide from it.

Step 2: Embrace And Master Your Emotions

It's important to understand that transforming fear into love isn't about repressing or denying the truth of your feelings. Mastering your emotions is a useful skill here; the thought is that you can fully embrace those emotions, acknowledge them, and find a way of processing them so they can be let go. Write in a journal, get them out through creative pursuits (such as painting or playing music), or channel them into physical endeavors like running, horse riding, dancing or boxing. This may seem counterintuitive, as you will be focusing on your fears. But sometimes facing your problems is important in order to finally let them go.

Find the courage to sit down and write down what has been worrying you. You will see that some fears are actually ridiculous when put on paper, and it will be easy for you to forget about them.

On the other hand, you might find fears that you didn't know existed. Don't worry, this is good. Many of us have fears that are eating us from the inside, but we've had them for so long that they became subconscious beliefs, and we don't even realize they exist. So, finding hidden fears is good, because once they are on the surface, you can start the process of letting them go.

Step 3: Demystify Your Fears

A lot of the power of fear comes from the fact that it's often poorly understood. For example, think about times you've experienced crawling unease, a pounding heart or a fear of failure without really having a grasp on exactly what frightens you or why.

To free up more space for love and reduce the potency of fear, deliberately seek to understand fear. Look straight at it, and begin to figure out its roots, what it represents, how it relates to your self-image, and so on.

In many cases, you'll uncover the limiting beliefs that often hold people back from using the Law of Attraction properly. Plus, you can use tools like affirmations and a focus wheel to replace those beliefs with positive, loving ones.

Step 4: Work On Letting Go Of Your Fears

Now, that your fears are no longer a secret, you can start eliminating them from your life. You have already made the first and most important step. You became conscious of your condition, and now you have the power to change your relationship with fear forever.

Step 5: Focus On Doing Good.

At the bottom, we all yearn to be heard, valued and truly seen by other people. Consequently, one of the most meaningful gestures you can make, is to just sit with another person and lend a non-judgmental ear to whatever they want to say. Provide empathy, work to understand them, and be fully present in the moment. This kind of love makes a world of difference to the other person, and it fills you with compassion. The next time you're feeling fearful, think of how you can offer love in this way, and shift your attention to doing just that.

Step 6: Associate A Special Object With Your Transformation

Just as you might have one specific item that you connect to your Law of Attraction goals, you can assign something similar to the related goal of turning fear into love. A small rock or stone is a common choice here, as you can hold it in the palm of your hand, imagining fear pouring into it and love pouring back out of it, soaking into your skin.
Other ideas include a piece of jewelry that you can wear, any time you need a reminder to focus on love (such as a heart pendant or a rose quartz ring) or a candle with a scent that makes you feel peaceful and steady.

Step 7: Stay Open

It's natural to shut down during times of fear, even if you're normally an open person. The next time you feel fear starting to undermine you, fight to keep your mind and heart open to possible courses of action.
Ask yourself what you can do to feel better in your current situation, take small but deliberate steps out of your comfort zone, and let other people care for you when they want to (instead of pushing them away). Don't isolate yourself or keep all your worries hidden; use your support network, and know there's no shame in making yourself vulnerable.

Step 8: Radiate Love.

One way of radiating love is to show compassion and understanding to those around you, as suggested above. However, it's not the only way. For example, you can try meditation exercises that involve imagining your heart sending out love to others; whether it's a community in need, a person experiencing sorrow, or just someone for whom you always wish the very best.

This simple act brings you in tune with abundance, putting you in the right place to manifest what you want to see in your future. In addition, consider the old idea of doing one random act of kindness every day.

Law of Attraction and Depression

As Law of Attraction experts often note, you attract what you send out into the world, and doing good things for strangers and friends alike helps you to attract much more goodness into your own life. If you suspect you are suffering from depression, it is always smart to discuss this with your doctor. Medication and therapy can offer routes to a happier life. However, it is also worth noting that the Law of Attraction can be a powerful ally in your journey towards better mental health.

If you have been diagnosed with depression and are already doing everything that your healthcare team has recommended, here are some of the best ways to use the Law of Attraction to combat depression. First of all, let yourself off the hook. The first thing you need to do is accept that you are dealing with a period of depression and that it will pass in time. If you beat yourself up for feeling low, you'll only feel worse and attract more negativity into your life. It's so important that you don't try to force yourself to feel differently. That could lead to an inauthentic way of being that won't help you manifest a happier life. However, avoid the opposite end of the spectrum as well; wallowing in melancholic feelings is distinct from accepting sadness. If you commit to a slow, steady process of treating yourself with non-judgmental kindness and building up your resilience, you can combat depression much more effectively. Set an intention to feel better, and do keep your eyes open for things that help you feel better. Let these improvements come naturally. Secondly, know you are still attracting positivity at the heart level. When you're depressed and yearning to use the Law of Attraction, you might worry that your low mood means you are constantly attracting more things to feel depressed about. However, you can feel safe in the knowledge that at the heart level, you are still attracting positive things. You want to feel better, but you're just not there yet. As a result, you may see positive developments manifest more slowly, but remind yourself that these changes can occur. Your heart is vibrating on a higher frequency and just waiting for the rest of you to start feeling better so that all of your various aspects can begin to work in harmony. Believing in this will help you in avoiding a vicious cycle of feeling bad that you're "not using the law of attraction properly". You are doing your best and just need a little more time!

Thirdly, meditate every day. Recent scientific studies show, a daily practice of meditation can work wonders when you're trying to boost your mental health. If you can only meditate for 5 minutes, that's a perfectly fine place to start. The key thing is to make time to meditate each day, gradually building up the amount of time you spend on it. Try a simple approach at first, such as focusing on your breath as you inhale and exhale, or staring at the flickering light of a candle's flame. Let stray thoughts pass by without close attention, knowing that you will attend to them later. When you're used to regular meditation, you can begin to use visualization techniques like imagining your heart filling with light. However, even the most basic meditation practice can help to combat depression by inducing feelings of peacefulness and calmness. You can also commit to regular, light exercise routines. Regularly doing some kind of light exercise helps to align your body with your heart's intentions to experience a shift in mood, creating conditions more conducive to overcoming depression.
When you exercise, your body releases endorphins—those feel-good hormones that lift your spirits and elevate your natural vibration in a way that supports your manifestation attempts. Good examples of gentle but effective exercise include swimming, walking, and relaxation yoga.
As with meditation, even ten minutes a day can help to change your emotional state, and you can gradually work up to 30 minutes or even an hour.
Finally, this tip is useful for anyone who wants to cultivate a more positive perspective and vibrate on a higher frequency, but it may be especially helpful if you're struggling with depression. Basically, think about all the negativity you get from the internet and TV; upsetting news, irritating dialogues, and reasons to feel envious or wonder if you're "good enough".
Try limiting your exposure to these negative influences, and take a more conscious, mindful approach to your online time.
Only tune into the things that genuinely make you feel happier or more inspired. And deliberately turn your attention to something else if you notice you're mindlessly browsing through social media.

Notice how your mental health can improve as a result, and consider a permanent change in habits if this approach is helping you manifest a more positive way of being.

By clearing the negativity from your daily life little by little, you will begin to see a transformation, and how things really are a lot easier than you previously believed them to be. You will also find you desire to remove even more of the limiting beliefs you possessed before about yourself and the way you lived your life, helping you to further discover and unlock your true potential. You'll also be clearing away the rest of your negative cobwebs and completely cutting the energetic cord to any other negative forces in your life.

CHAPTER FIVE
What the Mind Can Conceive, It Can Achieve

Do you find it hard to manifest the things you want into your life? Perhaps you follow the Law of Attraction and just can't quite conquer manifestation? It can be tricky at first, but once you get the hang of it, manifesting can become second nature to you. Maybe you are unsure of what manifestation really means. Or maybe you need clarity on what the purpose of manifestation is! In order to succeed in your manifestations, you need to truly believe in them.

So, it's worth knowing the ins and outs of what exactly manifestation is and how to properly manifest what you want. Before I share my guide with you, let's take a look at what it means and how it works.

What Does 'Manifestation' Mean?

There are many different 'definitions' of the word manifest, but the simplest would be that a manifestation is 'something that is put into your physical reality through thought, feelings, and beliefs'. This means that whatever you focus on is what you are bringing into your reality. You may focus and manifest through meditation, visualization or just via your conscious or subconscious. For example, if you have been thinking about getting a new job and you focused your thoughts and feelings on exactly what you wanted and when you wanted it, you could then try to meditate or visualize your goal and this can help to manifest it into your reality. If you then got your new job and it was everything you wanted, you would have successfully manifested it into your life. So, now that you know what manifestation means, it's time to find out how manifestation works.

How Does Manifestation Work?

As with the Law of Attraction, a manifestation is where your thoughts and your energies create your reality. If you are constantly being negative and feeling down, then you are going to attract and manifest negative energy. The first thing to do when manifesting is to take a look at your thoughts and feelings. Are you feeling negative? Do your thoughts surround negativity? If so, you could begin to manifest things you don't want in your reality. This

is why it's important to clear your mind and have a positive mindset when you are wanting to manifest.
Manifestation doesn't just work with your thoughts, there has to be a form of action on your part. This could be actually applying for the jobs that suit what you are looking for and going to the interviews. Visualizing your thoughts and feelings about your job will help you to feel more positive and motivated to make these changes a reality. This will then push you to take some action and, ultimately, manifest your goals into your life.

Step 1: Choose What You Want To Manifest

When you decide on something specific to manifest, it's vital that you know exactly why you want this specific thing in your life. And when you're trying to manifest something in just 24 hours, you also have to pick something you believe you can manifest in a day. So, for example, there's little point in saying you want to start a new business in 24 hours unless you actually believe you can attain this goal in the next day. However, you may well believe that you can successfully manifest the next step in your journey to a new business in a day, in which case you might set that as your goal (e.g. to complete a business plan, get a loan you need, or find someone to collaborate with).

When picking a thing to manifest, ask yourself the following questions:
* **Do I really want this, in my heart of hearts?**
* **How will I benefit from having this?**
* **When I think about having this, does it feel right?**
* **How will it be good for me and for others?**

Whatever you want should be for the greater good, and something you want in itself; most likely something that's a significant step on the journey towards a greater manifestation goal. So, in sum: decide what you want, really connect with the intention to have it, and believe that you will receive whatever it is you ask for.

Step 2: Get Rid Of Things That Stand In Your Way

Unfortunately, there will almost always be something standing in your way to success. This shouldn't scare you, this is just part of the whole manifestation process.

Keep an eye out for these three most common manifestation blocks:

* Negative beliefs/mindset

If you are in a bad place emotionally, you need to first get yourself into the right mindset before anything. You can't be focusing on negativity and expect to attract good things into your life. So take some time to practice self-care. Try meditation and different stress-relief techniques.

* Toxic people

When you are working on manifesting your dream ,you need to make sure no one is holding you back. People who don't believe in you, always criticize you and/or complain about everything are blocks that will keep you from doing your best.

* Timing

Sometimes you just need to be patient. Everything you want will happen, but it will happen at the right time and for the right reasons. So if something isn't happening for you right now, it doesn't mean it never will. Keep believing and keep working on your goal.
Sit back and think about how your manifestation process is going at the moment.
Do you feel like you're on the right path or is something holding you back from the prosperity, love, happiness, and abundance that you desire? Just wait it out. When in doubt, the best course of action is always to delay. Give the universe some time to process your order.

Step 3: Visualize What You Want To Manifest

You probably already know the basics of visualization, and have at least tried to practice those techniques a couple of times. On your current manifestation quest, start by going somewhere that's quiet and private, and spend just a minute on visualizing the thing you want.

Pour all your energy and concentration into seeing it with your mind's eye, and let all the good feelings about the object or outcome well up inside you.

This step works best if you do a multi-sensory visualization; if you can see, hear, smell, touch and (if relevant) taste the outcome you're looking to create. Make it as real as you possibly can, so it's almost like it's yours already. Never forget that phrase "Make it real". It should be your mantra, because that's what manifestation is all about, and the universe will work to support you in your cause.

Add as many details as you can, and don't try to imagine exactly how the thing or outcome becomes yours; instead, focus solely on the end result of receiving what you desire.

Don't think about how your desired object or outcome will manifest and don't try to see it coming to you through any particular person or means. Your focus should be on the end result of receiving the thing of your desire.

Step 4: Take Action To Manifest What You Want

You can spend the rest of your day pretty much living as you normally would; there isn't any particular action you need to take in order to make manifestation possible (your intentions are what will determine your success). Rather, once you've finished steps 1-2 as described above, you are just waiting for what you want to appear.

However, if you feel the urge to do something specific; whether it immediately makes sense or it's more of an intuition-based yearning. Then consider following your gut and taking that action. If it feels natural, do it! If you find that you don't get the outcome you want within 24 hours or less, look back at the first two steps and go back through them. Sometimes, writing down what you want (and some of the answers to the specific questions posed) can give the universe the extra nudge it needs to fuel your manifestation. There are some common reasons why you might not be manifesting quickly. In particular, consider whether you're doubting the process; do you either not believe you'll get what you ask for because you don't think you deserve it, or perhaps doubt whether it's possible to manifest using the Law of Attraction? Remember, any kind of negative feelings (e.g. anxiety, worry, anger, and doubt) or negative beliefs can inhibit your results.

Step 5: Recognize And Appreciate

Although this final step might not look that significant at first glance, it can actually do a lot to shape your manifestation potential in the future. Basically, the key thought here is that you need to fully appreciate what you have once you achieve your goal. It can be easy to forget that you asked for what you received, so take proactive steps to prevent this.

Go back to what you first thought and felt when you were visualizing your desired object or outcome, and connect those experiences with the new experience of having what you want. Consider the tangible proof you have that thoughts are things, and that thinking in a certain way can create concrete changes in the world around you.

The more you make this connection and emphasize it, the better you'll be at manifesting in the future (as you'll replace negative, limiting beliefs and doubts with confident, positive thoughts and feelings much easier).

CHAPTER SIX
On The Verge Of Manifestation?

So, you've finished all of our manifestation steps and you feel positive and motivated... now what? Well, as long as you can hold on to this feeling and stay positive, focus on your goals and take some form of action – then you've done all you can!
There are some signs that you should look out for in order to know your manifestation is close. It may feel like nothing has happened after you've set aside time to really think and feel your manifestations, but that's only the beginning.
These signs are likely to just appear to you, even if you aren't looking for them.

Signs Your Manifestation Is Close

When you are trying to manifest something into your life, there are many signs that you should be looking out for in order to know that your manifestation is close. Some will be small signs, and others might be staring you right in the face, without you knowing. Here are some of the signs that may come to you when your manifestation is close:
* **Hearing about your desires.** This could be overhearing someone's conversation or listening to the radio, where they are talking about the very thing that you want.
* **Feeling excited.** If you start to develop a sense of excitement despite there not being a reason, this could be a sign that your manifestation is close.
* **You see repeating numbers.** Repeating numbers have important meanings and these are a good sign that your manifestation is close. Pay attention to the numbers you see.
* **Other people talking about your goals.** The people in your life might bring up your goals in conversation, telling you that you would be good at something (even if they are unaware that this is your goal).
These are just a few signs to show that your manifestation is close to being in your reality. Make sure to keep note of the signs you are seeing.

CHAPTER SEVEN
Why Manifestation Is Not Working For You?

Do you need some extra help with your Law of Attraction journey? Maybe you feel that there is something that's holding you back? Using visualization techniques in your daily life can help to make the Law of Attraction much more real and powerful for you. It can help you map out an image in your head of everything you want out of life. Plus, it tells the universe what it is you would like to attract in your life. For example, if you would like a promotion in your job, visualize yourself moving into a new office, with your name on the door, and receiving a big check. What visualization does is help you to find your goals, focus and manifest them. This will then help you in creating a positive and motivated mindset.

Visualization involves creating images (which could be mental and physical) showing your goals and your future as a strong positive message. There are different tools and techniques which have been used by many successful people to achieve their goals and create their dream lives, all of which you can equally use to do the same. But first, let's take a look at why visualization is important.

Why Is Visualization Important?

There are various reasons why visualization is important and has many benefits too:

* **Strengthens your motivation.** Visualization helps you to feel motivated and excited to create your dream life.
* **Re-programs your brain.** Your visualization skills could help to re-program your brain into finding and recognizing pathways towards the manifestation your dreams and goals.
* **Confidence boost.** The more that you are visualize yourself achieving your goals and dreams, the more confidence you start to feel in yourself all round.
* **Stress relief.** When you are visualizing, you are normally in a calm state of mind. This calmness can help you to clear your mind, eliminating any worries and stresses you may have.

6 Easy And Effective Visualization Techniques

1. Dream Boards

A dream board (also known as a vision board) is a way of visually representing your aims, whether they're financial, romantic, spiritual or something else entirely.
Creating a dream board is an inexpensive and very creative way of connecting with your desires for the future. The dream boards can be made using everything from natural objects to drawings and magazine cutouts. When you create a vision board, you will be identifying your vision and dreams in a physical way as well as reinforcing your daily affirmations, which will be covered below.
     If you are looking for more inspiration on creating your own, you can explore more dream board examples and ideas. These vision boards need to be personal and unique to you; anything you find that motivates and inspires you should go on the board.
Your vision board is great to have in your office, or on the wall in your bedroom for example. You can have them there in the background keeping you motivated and operating within your subconscious.

2. Daily Affirmations

An affirmation is a simple statement that reshapes your beliefs and helps you move towards your life goals. Obviously, for this to work in your favor, they need to be positive affirmations.
An affirmation is a repeated and spoken statement. However, you can also include visual affirmations too. An example of a spoken, daily affirmation would be if you stand in front of your mirror and say to yourself 'I love having a great job and being happy in my own skin'. You would use this affirmation if you are trying to find a better job and maybe if you have low self-confidence and your goal is to feel happy with yourself.
     The Law of Attraction works on the basis that your thoughts and energies are recognized by the universe, which is why if you can put positive affirmations and energy out into the world, the universe will respond to it. Repetition plays a big part in your daily affirmations. The more that we tell ourselves something, the more the message is accepted by our self-conscious and can be manifested in our lives.

The idea of a visual affirmation is that there is a physical concrete form of your affirmation.

Examples of these would be:

* Having your affirmations on signs and put up where you can always see them. It may also be a good idea to have your visual affirmation stuck near the area connected to your goals, such as a mirror, if you are looking to improve your self-image and self-worth.
* Set up reminders on your phone, so that your affirmation regularly appears in front of you. This can also be set as an alarm so that you have daily reminders each morning or before you sleep.
* Repeatedly write out your affirmations at the beginning or end of the day. This can also connect with a gratitude journal, which is covered below.

3. Meditation

Meditation is a great visualization technique as you are using visualization at a time that your mind is clear and present. When you meditate, you start to gain access to your inner self more than you probably ever have. As you will be fully present in that moment, you can truly focus on yourself and your goals and aspirations. You can use this time whilst meditating to visualize your goals, create a positive space and send out positive energy. Meditating helps your brain release any negative energy. It also gives your brain the space to go wherever it wants, which is why this is very helpful when visualizing. You should be able to have strong visualizations through meditation, as you are allowing your brain to do the work for you, whilst letting any negative energy go.

4. Gratitude Journal

A gratitude journal is a great visualization tool that can help you to believe in your success and goals while also providing you with a positive mindset. A gratitude journal is where you write down everything that you are grateful for that day (if you are doing this daily – which we recommend!).

Each night before you sleep, write down 5-10 things that you were grateful for that day. Doing this keeps you in a positive mindset and makes you reflect on the good things in your life. By concentrating on creating a happy present experience, you also teach yourself to expect the most from your future. This will help you to visualize your future, in a positive and meaningful way.

You can also look back at what you have been grateful for and take as many useful lessons and positives messages from them as possible. Reflecting on the good things about yourself and your life from your gratitude journal enhances your belief that you can, and deserve to, reach your goals.

4. Magic Check

Another great visualization tool is to use what is called a Magic Check (also known as dream check). You can use this to attract wealth or financial freedom as well as much more.

The idea of this is to have a self-written check that is made out to you and clearly states what you want to achieve. This could be financial, but it could also be a goal such as landing a new job or finding your ideal partner.

A dream check is best put somewhere that you will constantly see it. This could be next to your bed or even in your purse. As mentioned, the dream check does not always have to be about finances if you don't want it to. Whatever your goal is, write it on the check and make sure you feel good about what you are trying to manifest.

Fuel your check with as much positivity as possible and pretend that you have already received this sum of money or goal that you want to achieve.

5. Creative Visualization

Get creative with your visualization! Even if you are not an artsy person, you will be surprised to find how impactful it is to create art that visually represents your dreams. You can do this by painting, drawing, writing or even creating graphics on your computer. Some people will find this visualization technique better, as they have a creative outlet for their goals and dreams. Just like a vision board, you can hang your art somewhere you can always see it. In fact, creating the art yourself will only make it more personal and unique to you.

CHAPTER EIGHT
Law of Attraction Exercises

The Law of Attraction is no scary science or heavy philosophy – it is all about turning good intentions into positive action. It really is as simple as that. Simple exercises like filling your thoughts, words, and energies with positivity and possibility, knowing exactly what it is that you want and then simply 'allowing' the universe to flow. It doesn't matter if you are new to the Law of Attraction, a number one fan of the universal laws or the world's biggest skeptic; if you would love nothing more than to master the Law of Attraction and add a little positivity to your day, or find out what it could do for you – here are a few simple exercises to get you started.

1. Treat The Universe Like Your Personal Supermarket

Make your very own 'manifesting shopping list'. Every day, no matter where you go, scribble out lists of what you want from the universe.
Write them on your phone, on scraps of paper or in a beautiful notebook bought specifically for the task. Writing lists like this will help you to get really clear on what it is that you want.
However, the biggest advantage of this exercise is that the more you lose and forget about your lists, the easier it will become for these things to manifest in your life.
When we focus really hard on waiting for something to show up in our lives, our energies can become ones of worry and 'lack' – creating resistance.
So, once we have gotten clarity on what it is that we want and forgotten about our lists, we let our dreams go. This takes all pressure off of the manifesting process, leaving our dreams in the hands of the universe.
Other exercises that embrace your creative visualizations also include using a vision board, creating a focus wheel or even writing a dream journal.

2. Play Make Believe

Taking some time out to play in the realms of your imagination with creative visualization exercises, can prove a fun and simple exercise for raising your feel-good vibrations.

Plus, it helps to tell the universe exactly what it is you wish to manifest in your life.

Try spending 10-15 minutes imagining how your perfect day would go. What would you be doing? What would you look like? Who would you spend your time with? Enjoy exploring the life that you know you are in the process of creating.

3. Manifest Something

Practice manifesting something small, to give yourself confidence and help hone your creative capabilities. Begin by trying to manifest something small and even insignificant – it could be anything from a distinctive flower to a book. You want to start small as you need something that you have no resistance to, something you feel no pressure to manifest.

Now, spend a couple of minutes thinking about this item. How will you feel when you have it? How will it feel in your hand? Just relax and let it fill your thoughts for a few moments.

Last but not least, forget about it. Let it go, and rather than worry about whether this thing will show up or not, look forward to it unexpectedly popping up in your life.

Simple beginners' practices such as these can help to raise your frequency and bring your mind to a place of positivity and better alignment with your goals.

Further still, as evidence of the Law of Attraction begins to crop up in your day-to-day life your confidence will begin to grow, until you are able to begin manifesting even bigger and greater things.